OPPOSITES

4880 Lower Valley Road, Atglen, PA 19310

MOON

THE SILVERY MOON SHIVERS, SEEMINGLY AWARE
OF THE WOLVES THAT ARE HOWLING IN THE COLD MORNING AIR.

SUN

THE GOLDEN SUN SHINES, BRIGHT AS A PYRE.
THE PLANTS DRINK IN ITS SACRED FIRE.

THE BLEND OF MOON AND SUN
MAKES FOR A DAWN WHOSE BEAUTY
CAN'T BE OUTDONE.

AIM FOR THE MOON.
IF YOU MISS, YOU MAY HIT A STAR.

—W. CLEMENT STONE
AMERICAN BUSINESSMAN AND WRITER

RIVER

THE FREEZING WATER FINDS A WAY ON ITS QUEST,
RUSHING TOWARD THE BEACH, ITS DREAM UNEXPRESSED.

MOUNTAIN

THE EARTH RISES SPLENDIDLY TOWARD THE SKY,
HOPING, JUST HOPING, TO TOUCH A STAR ON HIGH.

THE MIX OF MOUNTAIN AND RIVER
IS THE SNOW-CAPPED PEAK WHEN THE SUN MAKES IT QUIVER.

WATER, WHERE DO YOU GO?
DOWN THE RIVER I GO LAUGHING
TO THE SHORES OF THE SEA.

—FEDERICO GARCÍA LORCA
SPANISH POET

SKY

YOU ARE THE CANOPY OF THE PLANET.
AN IMMENSE VIOLET DOME,
DREAMS AND COMETS, THEY CALL YOU HOME.

EARTH

YOU ARE THE PLANET'S TAPESTRY,
A HUGE FIREBALL TURNED TO STONE,
WHERE NEW, PRECIOUS LIFE HAS SINCE GROWN.

THE MIX OF EARTH AND SKY
IS THE WIND MAKING THE LEAVES DANCE AND FLY.

"COME TO THE EDGE," HE SAID.
"WE CAN'T—WE'RE AFRAID!" THEY RESPONDED.
"COME TO THE EDGE," HE REPEATED.
AND SO THEY CAME.
AND HE PUSHED THEM . . . AND THEY FLEW.

—CHRISTOPHER LOGUE
BRITISH POET

WINTER

MY SWEATER AND WOOL HAT KEEP OUT THE COLD AIR.
I SEE HOW THE SEASON HAS LAID BRANCHES BARE.
THE FIRE DANCES AT HOME, CALLING ME THERE.

SUMMER

UNDER THE SHADE OF MY
WIDE-BRIMMED STRAW HAT,
I SEE THE PURPLE FRUIT ON
THE TREES GROW FAT.
MAKING JAM AT HOME,
THERE'S NOTHING BETTER
THAN THAT!

THE WINTER AND SUMMER, WHEN THEY BLEND,
BECOME THE SPRING'S COLORS WITH NO END,
AND THE GOLDEN FALL WHEN THE LEAVES DESCEND.

ANYTHING ESSENTIAL IS INVISIBLE TO THE EYES.
... IT'S THE TIME THAT YOU SPENT ON YOUR ROSE
THAT MAKES YOUR ROSE SO IMPORTANT.

—ANTOINE DE SAINT-EXUPÉRY, *THE LITTLE PRINCE*
FRENCH AVIATOR AND WRITER

SILENCE

OH WHERE, OH WHERE DID THE SILENCE HIDE AWAY?
FOR WHEN I CALLED TO IT, NOT A WORD DID IT SAY.

SOUND

BEHIND EVERY SOUND, IT CROUCHES AND IT WAITS.
I DISCOVER THE SILENCE WHEN THE NOISE DISSIPATES.

THE MIX OF SILENCE AND SOUND
IS A CAT PURRING ON THE FOREST GROUND.

THE AIR WAS FULL OF ALL THE NIGHT NOISES
THAT, TAKEN TOGETHER, MAKE ONE BIG SILENCE.

—RUDYARD KIPLING, *THE JUNGLE BOOK*
BRITISH WRITER

WATER

THE RAIN AND THE SEAGULL PLAY.
CRYSTALLINE WATER FALLS FROM THE SKY SO GRAY.
HERE IN THE EARTH, WITH NO TRACE OF FEAR,
SOAKS A NEW SEED, READY FOR ITS PREMIERE.

FIRE

IN THE KITCHEN, THE FLAMES BURN BRIGHT.
ITS LIGHT WARMS US AND HELPS US SEE IN THE NIGHT.
FIRE SPEAKS WITH A VOICE FROM CENTURIES PAST
OF LIFE, INFINITY, AND THE UNIVERSE SO VAST.

THE MIX OF WATER AND FIRE
MAKES THE CLOUDS FLOAT EVER HIGHER.

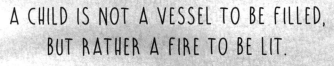

A CHILD IS NOT A VESSEL TO BE FILLED,
BUT RATHER A FIRE TO BE LIT.

—PLUTARCH
GREEK PHILOSOPHER

BEAUTY

WE'VE ALL HEARD OF THE BEAUTY OF ITS WINGS.
THE COLORS OF THE SKY, FIT FOR A BANQUET OF KINGS.
BLUES, ORANGES, YELLOWS, AND PINKS IT BRINGS.

UGLINESS

THEY TOLD ME IT WAS SO UGLY, IT MIGHT SCARE ME AWAY.
ITS COLORS WERE DULL AND IT CRAWLED EVERY WHICH WAY.
POOR CATERPILLAR—NO ONE KNEW WHAT YOU'D BE SOMEDAY.

MIXING THE TWO, UGLINESS AND BEAUTY,
SEEMS TO BE NATURE'S SACRED DUTY.

HE NO LONGER WANTED TO BE THE GREATEST,
STRONGEST, OR CLEVEREST.
HE HAD LEFT ALL THAT FAR BEHIND.
HE LONGED TO BE LOVED JUST AS HE WAS,
GOOD OR BAD, HANDSOME OR UGLY, CLEVER OR STUPID,
WITH ALL OF HIS FAULTS . . .
OR POSSIBLY BECAUSE OF THEM.

— MICHAEL ENDE, *THE NEVERENDING STORY*
GERMAN WRITER

CALM

THE OCEAN LOOKS LIKE A MIRROR, BRIGHT OUT ON THE BAY.
WHERE IT ENDS AND THE HEAVENS BEGIN, WHO IS TO SAY?

STORM

THE HORIZON IS EVER MORE FRIGHTENING.
WHEN WILL THEY BE OVER, THE THUNDER AND LIGHTNING?

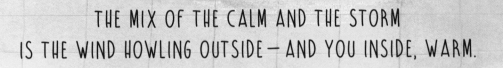

THE MIX OF THE CALM AND THE STORM
IS THE WIND HOWLING OUTSIDE—AND YOU INSIDE, WARM.

AFTER THE RAIN, THE SUN WILL REAPPEAR. THERE IS LIFE.
AFTER THE PAIN, THE JOY WILL STILL BE HERE.
—WALT DISNEY
AMERICAN ILLUSTRATOR AND FILM PRODUCER

EMOTION

PASSIONATE AND FREE,
FEEL THE MAGIC INSIDE YOU AND ME.

REASON

THINKING, PRECISE,
HELPING US TO SOLVE
THE MYSTERIES OF LIFE.

"ALL THE SAME," SAID THE SCARECROW,
"I SHALL ASK FOR BRAINS INSTEAD OF A HEART;
FOR A FOOL WOULD NOT KNOW WHAT TO DO
WITH A HEART IF HE HAD ONE."
"I SHALL TAKE THE HEART," RETURNED THE TIN WOODMAN;
"FOR BRAINS DO NOT MAKE ONE HAPPY,
AND HAPPINESS IS THE BEST THING IN THE WORLD."

—L. FRANK BAUM, *THE WONDERFUL WIZARD OF OZ*
AMERICAN WRITER

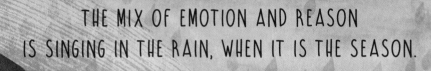

THE MIX OF EMOTION AND REASON
IS SINGING IN THE RAIN, WHEN IT IS THE SEASON.

FEMININE ENERGY

IT FLOATS BETWEEN PETALS, THEN IN REPOSE.
SOFT, WEIGHTLESS, AND GENTLE IT GOES.
OH, TO FEEL THE CALM IT KNOWS.

MASCULINE ENERGY

THROUGH THE VALLEY IT RUNS, UNTAMED.
QUICK AND STRONG AND HARDLY CONTAINED,
IT HOLDS WITHIN A POWER UNNAMED.

FREE TO BE YOU AND ME.

— RUTH BADER GINSBURG
AMERICAN JUDGE AND WRITER,
INVOKING A SONG BY MARLO THOMAS

MASCULINE AND FEMININE ENERGY COMBINED
IS TO RUN AND THEN REST IN THE SHADE THAT WE FIND.

DEATH

THE FRUIT FALLS HEAVY ON THE GRASS.
WITHERING, SHRINKING, TO DUST IT SHALL PASS.
IN SILENCE, THE SEEDS WILL WAIT
FOR SPRING TO COME AND REVEAL THEIR FATE.

LIFE

A BLADE OF GRASS PEEKS OUT,
FRESH AND NEW FROM
THE EARTH DOES IT SPROUT.
ITS TENDER YOUNG HEART BEATING,
FULLY AT EASE,
FEELS TO US LIKE A
WARM SUMMER'S BREEZE.

DEATH AND LIFE, WHEN UNITED,
OFFER THE CHANCE TO HAVE OUR STRENGTH IGNITED.